The Disney Experience

Work Hard, Play Hard

Christian Lawrence

DEDICATION

This book is dedicated to the students who are looking to do the Disney College Program, those who have completed the Disney College Program, and those who would like to get a glimpse of what the program has to offer.

This book is especially dedicated to the participants of the Fall 2012 Disney College Program.

CONTENTS

INTRODUCTION

Walt Disney World - *the place where dreams come true*. While many of us think about the memories created by families and their amazing children, there are also memories created by aspiring, young professionals who make those dreams come true.

Walt Disney World offers an internship for students called the "Disney College Program". This program allows students from all around the world to come to either Walt Disney World (Orlando, Florida) or Disneyland (Anaheim, California). While on the program, you are placed into Disney sponsored housing with other students that have the same arrival/departure date for the program. It also offers the chance to take special collegiate classes that some colleges count as credit for the students.

The extensive training and preparation that Disney provides these amazing and talented individuals is very superior compared to other companies. Once you arrive, it's training, training, and more training. It's no wonder why Disney is known for having the best guest service in the world!

As for myself, I took on two of these programs at Walt Disney World. My first program was in Fall 2012, and my last was Spring 2014. Throughout both of these programs, I discovered new things about myself, created lifelong friendships and had the journey of a lifetime. Disney will forever hold a place in my heart for changing my life and making me a better person.

My goal of this book is to inform readers what it is that happens on the program, what you learn, and how life changing this amazing experience can be.

1 ARRIVING

Many people who make their way to Florida leave a few days early before their program begins to ensure they have enough time to get a comfortable feel for their new home. For me, I lived in North Carolina. My GPS told me I was a good 8 hours away from my destination which was a Holiday Inn Express hotel located in the Lake Buena Vista, Florida area. My drive down there wasn't that bad, but my nerves were completely shot. Never had I moved away from home this far away and the thought of not knowing anyone scared me. The only thing I had to look forward to my first night in Orlando was meeting my roommate, Manuel, who I met on Facebook a month in advance to be my roommate.

Upon arriving for your program, I recommend you book a hotel in the Lake Buena Vista area. If you're like me, you've never heard of this city, but it is one. It's a small, yet busy town that Disney pretty much owns and operates. (Not really, but you get the idea). For both of my programs, I stayed at the Holiday Inn Express which has an Applebee's Restaurant attached to it. I recommend this because many programs have a meet and greet (pre-arrival) gathering at that Applebee's. I hosted my programs arrival party for Spring 2014 and found many students were staying at that hotel as well. This Holiday Inn is also located just a few steps away from where you will be checking in for your program. If you find that you cannot book this hotel, there are other good options in the Celebration, Florida area.

Disney will give you a specific time to be in line at the Vista Way Apartment Complex. This is the time that you take your picture for the Housing ID Card, and get the keys to your new apartment! It's really exciting. If you are alone when you are in line, don't be shy. Join in on conversations and introduce yourself. You're at Disney! Be proud and be happy. Honestly, the waiting in line gets pretty long (could be more than an hour) so make the most out of your time and mingle!

OVERALL TIPS FOR ARRIVING:

• If you plan to arrive early for your program, **book your hotel in advance** as they fill up quickly.

• Holiday Inn Express (13351 State Rd 535 Orlando, FL, 32821) is your best bet if you want to be close for your program check in, and **meet other program participants**!

• **Don't over pack** - You will be working many, many hours. Don't bring everything you own. Depending on when you're arriving, it can get cold in Orlando. Seriously. Late November, December, January, and February are all chilly depending on what you think chilly is. The good news is it does warm up fast after February, so pack your clothes accordingly.

• Try to find your program's **Facebook group**. (Ex. Disney College Program Fall 2012). This is a good way to meet other people in your same program.

• If you have a car, drive around the area and become comfortable. **Learn where the important places are**.

2 SETTLING

Disney housing includes three different apartment complexes.

- Vista Way
- Chatham Square
- Patterson Court

Despite what you may have already read or heard about these complexes, some of it may or may not be true, so let me clear that up right now.

VISTA WAY:
Vista Way is the oldest of the three complexes. I never wanted to stay in them because of what I heard, but when I got placed in Vista for Spring 2014, I actually loved it and would prefer Vista if I had to do it again. Though the complex is old, it's very comfortable and convenient. Vista Way is Disney's transportation hub. If you ever need a ride, you're two steps away from always catching a ride, for free! The busses go to every complex, but because Vista is the hub, there's always a

bus to catch! Out of all three complexes, Vista is closest to Disney and there's a Wendy's, Chic-Fil-A, and Walgreens right in front of the complex. If you don't have a car, this is a good place to be for sure.

CHATHAM SQUARE:

Chatham is nice. I stayed in a 1 bedroom unit on my first program in 2012. I really can't complain about anything in the complex. It was a good, quiet time and that's probably the most important factor - quiet. Vista is known for loudness because party busses come and go all the time. Chatham has a nice reputation for quietness, but also having fun at the same time. It's a good balance if you think about it. The kitchen is nice, has marble top counters, and the balcony is spacious.

PATTERSON COURT:

Patterson is very nice, and though I never lived in Patterson, it's the nicest out of the three complexes. It's really upscale, and I highly suggest staying here for anyone taking any of the classes offered by Disney. Many of the classes are held in Patterson, but just make sure first. The pool is spectacular, and overall, the feel of Patterson makes you feel like you're in a 5 star setting. The inside is nice. I preferably like Chatham's interior better, but I rank Patterson #1 for every other category.

APARTMENT PRICING:

Vista is the cheapest, followed by Chatham, and then Patterson. If you're on a budget with limited funds and want to save money, live in Vista. If you want to live in a very nice complex and pay for it, choose Chatham or Patterson. Either way, your rent is deducted WEEKLY out of your paycheck. The difference in paying $88 weekly, or $110 weekly might not sound like much, but it adds up quickly. Do your budget and choose what you feel more financially able to handle. Also, note that the more roommates you have, the less you pay for weekly rent. If you have one roommate, you pay a lot more, and if you have a house of eight people, you pay a lot less.

Chatham and Patterson are both furthest away from Disney. If you have a car, and plan on driving to work, leaving a little early will be ideal. If you work at Magic Kingdom, leaving for work more than an hour early is not unusual. Once you know where it will be, try and make some time to travel to your work location to get an idea of how long it will take you to get to work every day.

So, moving in is actually really fun. Even if you don't know who your roommates are prior to arriving, this is one thing Disney will teach you over time. DIVERSITY. Not everyone is going to be the same as you, and not everyone is going to like the same things as you. The biggest thing I can stress to those who are going to do a program is to be open-minded. We're all here to be a part of the magic that Disney creates, and that's all that matters. Race, color, religion, sex, age, whatever - none of that matters at Disney! If you unlock your apartment door and see you're the first one there, go ahead and choose a room. First come, first serve. It's fair. On my last program, in Spring 2014, I was the last to arrive and had to settle for the last open spot. When people arrive, make them feel welcome, and offer to help bring their belongings in.

So, you can have as little as 1 roommate, or as many as 8. Though having one roommate may have changed since I was there in 2012, the point is you will more than likely be having at least 4 roommates (including you).

Regardless of which apartment complex you're residing at, many participants find it easier to assign cabinet space in the kitchen. We all have different eating habits. For me, my spaces were the two cabinets above the stove. It wasn't ample room, but it was enough to store my Raman and canned foods. As far as the fridge and freezer, that space is shared and you can't divide that up. (I mean, you could but no one really did that during my program). Communication is key when having roommates. Before you make any decisions about where to put your stuff, talk it over with everyone and come to an agreement. Some people don't care and have a free for all policy which means anyone is welcome to whatever they want. But, if you're like me, and you're on a budget with limited funds, you probably won't like that concept!

The first night you're in your new apartment, arrange (if possible) for a night out on the town. Downtown Disney is very popular and has many things for you to do. This is the perfect time to go out with your roommates and get to know them on a more personal level. Some people like to go and do their own thing, but just know that when your training starts, you will rarely see your roommates. It does get very busy once work starts, so plan your time accordingly!

Your beds are small. For me, I'm tall and so my feet would always hang off the end of the bed. I got used to it, but don't expect a king/queen style living! If you go to Walmart and get a memory foam pad for a decent price, and a nice comforter, you sleep pretty well. Many of the beds squeak when you move or turn over. It's kind of annoying, but you get used to it, I promise! Also, some people like to bring or buy bed risers. I didn't use them, but the beds are low to ground.

OVERALL TIPS FOR MOVING IN:

• Think about your **budget** before choosing your complex.

• **Consider your lifestyle** – are you a highly social person? Vista way would be ideal for you.

• **Don't try to get in line early**. They will send you back (most of the time). Plan to arrive, in line, at the time Disney has provided you.

• **Discuss** the food/kitchen arrangements with ALL your roommates before making any decisions.

3 DISCOVERING

The most exciting part about your first few days of being at Disney is that moment when you discover what you will be doing on your program. If you remember, during your phone interview, you were asked about the different roles you were interested in. Don't worry! Disney has a nice, fun way of telling you what your role will be. I don't want to spoil it for you! But, on my first program, I was given Main Entrance Operations - Parking Support at Epcot. On my second program, I was given Merchandise - Retail at Epcot (Future World North).

No matter what your role in the show is, please do NOT get discouraged if it's something you didn't expect, or something you find out you don't enjoy. I promise you it gets better. During my first couple days at work doing parking, I absolutely hated it. I was in a huge parking lot, standing under the sun at over 100 degrees, burning, and using my hands to guide cars into the park. Do you think I wanted to hang it up and call it a day? Yeah, you dang right! I thought about it so many times, but you know what? I didn't quit. I never gave up. I went and talked to my leaders and looked for support and guidance. I made them aware of my situation and told them I wasn't enjoying my experience. They worked with me, and guided me along the way to be better and to appreciate what I really had going for me. Even at a later time, I had disagreements with a fellow cast member, and because I spoke up and sought that guidance, Disney fixed it. They really do care for you and want to see you succeed on your college program.

4 TRAINING

Work hard, play hard, remember? That's what the book was called. Well, it's true. Once you get into the training, it's on! After working for many companies, I've never seen anyone take as much pride and energy into their training like Disney does. You can't just be the happiest place on earth and hire anyone to provide the magic. That's why the magic begins with you. You were chosen to help make the magic, and Disney provides you with the resources to make that happen. You will get classroom training to learn about the history of the company, learn about the culture, and what it means to really make Disney magic. You will also interact with other participants in games, trivia, and more to get a feel for what the job itself will be like. Once you complete the classroom training, you will eventually move on to OTJ Training, or on the job training. This is the time where you meet with your area trainer at a location provided to you by Disney. Once you meet your trainer, they will take you to get your new costume! Yes, costume! Make sure you don't call it a uniform because they will ding you for that. You wear a costume because you're part of a show!

During this type of training, you will be with your trainer performing various jobs that your role requires. When I was doing my training for parking, I had to train on driving the parking tram, talking on the back of it, guiding cars to park in the parking lot and crowd controlling. Once you have successfully completed your training and complete all of the assessments, you will be on your own to create the magic. Generally, training only takes a week or so. Ask many questions and remember, there is no such thing as a bad question!

5 LIVING

The Disney College Program is all about three different components. Living, learning, and earning. It's very important to take all three components seriously to have a very good and enjoyable program. Here, we'll discuss the first one, living.

As mentioned before, you have your three different apartment complexes. Vista, Chatham and Patterson. One of the biggest things to know and prepare for are the housing inspections. Your monthly housing inspections shouldn't be a surprise. Disney doesn't want people to live in a trashy and messy place. Because of this, your complex and your unit will undergo monthly inspections. Two inspectors enter your room on a given day (you will have a heads up on what week it will be, just not the time) and will spend less than 5 minutes going through your apartment. Here are some of the things that they heavily look at.

- **Fire Hazards** - Candles, grills outside, etc.
- **Cleanliness of the bathroom**
  - Toilet - yes, someone needs to clean it
  - Sink – when you shave, make sure you rinse the sink out
  - Shower - make there is no mold or mildew
- **Cleanliness of the kitchen**
  - Trash needs to be emptied. Even if it's half full, they will ding you for it.
  - Dishes need to be put away, and not in the sink.
  - Kitchen floor needs to be cleaned/mopped
- **Bedroom clutter**
  - Basically things need to be clear from the door (but the cleaner, the better)
  - The safer everything is, the better

They have a pretty hefty checklist on them. As long as you make sure the above items are taken care of, you're in good shape. If you fail, everyone in the apartment has to pay a fee and they will come back to do another inspection. It's not worth losing money because you have an unsanitary apartment. 'Clean as you go' was the biggest thing people emphasized on my previous programs. It may sound elementary, but it works!

There is usually that ONE roommate who is either hard to get along with, or just doesn't like to do what everyone else agrees to do. If this were to ever happen to you, don't panic. If you (and/or your roommates) take solid attempts to try and fix the situation, and there's no way it's working, Disney Housing will step in and mediate the problem. Most of the time, the one causing the issues will get replaced or in severe cases, terminated and sent home. Every complex has a housing center that's open during normal business hours. Feel free to drop by if you ever have an issue with a roommate that isn't getting resolved. We all want to have a great time, and no one needs to ruin that for the rest of us!

6 LEARNING

Disney offers many courses that, while optional, will greatly benefit your future career whether you decide to stay with Disney or not. These courses (at the time of writing this book) include the following:

- Advanced Studies in Hospitality Management
- Corporate Communications
- Creativity & Innovation: Gaining the Edge
- Experiential Learning
- Human Resource Management
- Interactive Learning Program
- Organizational Leadership

I successfully completed the Human Resource Management course during my first college program. My classes were every Friday at 8:00am. I know, very early. But, I wanted to sacrifice the time I would be sleeping to actually learn something that was relevant to my major.

I loved this class. It was very interesting, and even with majoring in Human Resources, I learned a lot more in this ONE class than I did from some of the ones I took in college. The class was just like any other college class, but there was a difference. Each class is tailored around the Disney way and the Disney culture. Not only did I learn about HR in my class, but I learned about Disney's HR. I was able to learn about how Disney recruits, the different pay scales in the company, and more. Also, might I add, if you ever have any aspirations for a professional internship with Disney, they love the ones who take *at least* one of these classes. It's also another way to get involved, socially, and meet other participants!

Unfortunately, my university didn't grant me credit for this class, but I did get a full time credit notation on my transcript for financial aid purposes. On paper, it still showed I was full time in school, even though I was at Disney. This allowed me to get a student refund check for a pretty huge amount that I was able to have during my first program. If you ever have any questions about that, you can reach out to me and I will try to answer any questions you may have!

One last thing before we move on. If you decide to enroll in one of these classes, Disney requires your work location to give you that day off. So, if you want to always have off Fridays, take a Friday class. Even if like me, you have to get up early, at least you're off the whole day! Also, some locations give you back to back days off (not all). Just something to keep in mind while you decide on what class to take and on what day.

7 EARNING

The question that most people have is how much am I getting paid, and when do I get paid? Well, generally most participants will get paid minimum wage for Florida. Though your wage varies depending on what your role is, generally lifeguards get paid a higher wage than most. Don't panic, though. We're all in college, and making minimum wage does seem scary. I know. On my first program, I left a job making $10.00/hr to come down here. Wait, you think that's bad? After I actually *graduated* college, and landed a nice HR job making $36,000 a year, you know what I did? Yep, you guessed it. I came right on back to Disney. A lot of people thought I was crazy for doing that, but I knew it would be worth it. I don't want to tell you to leave your current job so please don't think I'm telling you that! But, just know people have done it before and it's all about deciding what is best for you. If you have a lot of financial responsibilities, this may not the best thing for you to do. But, if you like taking risks and you're all about that high risk, high reward, you might as well give it a shot. Here's a snapshot of how the earning works on the Disney College Program.

- Most participants earn minimum wage for Florida
- Overtime is 1.5x your pay over 40 hours
- Overtime is paid for time worked over 8 hours in one shift.
  - If you work a 12 hour shift, 8 hours are paid your normal rate, and 4 hours are OT.
- Double time is paid (2x your pay) for any shift you work that is less than 8 hours from your previous shift.
  - If you got off at midnight, and had to work at 7:00am that next morning, that entire shift you work is double your pay
- No limit on your hours.
  - You can pick up shifts from other people as long as you don't go over 40 hours
  - But you can pick up shifts on Disney's internal site at no limit.

During the holidays, and peak times, more shifts pop up on Disney's internal shift pickup website, also known as The Hub. For Christmas 2012, I actually had 78 hours in one week. Do the math and it's not a bad paycheck!

There are some deductions, obviously. Your housing rent comes out of your check on a weekly basis. If for some reason you are unable to meet that amount in a certain paycheck, it will come out of your next one until it's paid off. There's no way to get out of paying it.

For taxes, Florida doesn't have state income tax. Keep this in mind when you do your taxes for the following year. If your home state (that you reside) has state income tax, you will have to pay back your home state for the income tax you weren't taxed in Florida.

Lastly, you get paid every Thursday. You can remember that by EPCOT. (Every paycheck comes on Thursday)

8 SOCIALIZING

On my 2nd college program, many people I gave this advice to didn't believe me until they realized it later down the road. That advice was to make the most out of the time you have to meet and develop bonds with people. Go out, have fun, and again - work hard, play hard. But I want to emphasize one important thing. The people you meet before you start work (people you meet at a pre-arrival party, at check-in, etc.) are the ones that you MIGHT develop lifelong friendships with. If you want my advice, the ones you really need to develop with the most are the ones you work with in your area. 100% of college program participants will tell you the people they worked with on their program made it that much better. To be blunt, almost all of your jobs regardless of your role will get boring and dry. The friendships you make at work will make life easier and more pleasing.

On my first program, the managers in my area (at the end of our program) were shedding tears because they never had a group of participants who bonded as much as we did. We were more than work friends. We all went out after work to grab food, or see a movie, or even go to House of Blues (will describe more later). There's nothing like coming into work and seeing the same people you had a blast with the night before. It actually will increase your production at work and you will feel happier. The happier you are, the better service you give to the guests! It all works out in the end.

For those who enjoy socializing and going out, read on. At Downtown Disney, there is a wonderful place called House of Blues. EVERY Sunday night, this venue turns into an electronic, laser lighted, bass dropping, foggy extravaganza. Disney College Program participants (CP's) get in for free if you're over 21. Even if you're not 21, you can still get in! While it is a lot of fun to go with people from work, feel free to go with whoever you know is going. Before stepping into this place, I was not a huge fan of clubs, or large crowds, but House of Blues changed my perception and now every time I go visit, I always have to make sure my Sunday nights are blocked out just for House of Blues. Just give it a shot. If you don't like it, don't ever go again. But, at least try it one time to say you did!

Your roommates will also be a good go-to if you ever want to go out and explore. Park hopping is a fun activity to do on your days off. Everyone gets in for free, so it is possible to make a day fun without spending money if you are on a budget!

Whatever you do, don't go through your program without socializing. Find the people you are comfortable with, hang out with them and have fun. This is a once in a lifetime opportunity. When you look back at this moment after your program, you will be thankful you did, I promise!

OVERALL TIPS FOR SOCIALIZING:

- Work hard, yes, but also PLAY hard!
- Really get to know your fellow interns in your work area
- House of Blues (Disney College Program night – Every Sunday night)
    - Best time to arrive is after 11pm. The venue closes at 2am
- Even if you consider yourself anti-social, find something to do with people. There ARE people you will meet that you will want to be around!

9 NETWORKING

For those of you who are business minded and like to shake hands, listen up. This is the best time to let people know who you are. Being on the college program is your first step in the door for working at Disney one day in the future if that's what you want to do. Disney will send out emails every once in a while letting you know about upcoming networking events. Please take advantage of these events if you can, even if you have to switch shifts with someone or talk to your managers about schedule changes. Some of these events can include resume building seminars, career guidance and more. At all of these events, find time (after the event) to go up and introduce yourself to the panelists. Here are some tips when you do this:

- Dress your best for career success
- Use a **firm** handshake
- Make **direct eye contact** when communicating
- Ask them questions about their past experiences
- Let them know your aspirations
- Inform them of your major

- Ask them for a card
  - THIS IS IMPORTANT. Ask for their business card and keep in touch. What I found to be most rewarding is finding them on LinkedIn and adding them as a connection.
  - Also, send them an email every once in a while and let them know how you're doing and ask about possible job shadowing for your area.

Now, aside from the networking events, make use of your managers in your work location. These are your GSMs, or Guest Service Managers. They are the ones you go to for schedule conflicts, or if you have any questions about anything pertaining to your location. Make sure you get their business card and email addresses. Because you are going to see them nearly every day, make them your best friends. Below are some tips when networking with your GSMs.

- Greet them with a smile every time you see them
- What is your major? Ask them who they know that works in the area that relates to your major.
- Ask them about becoming a trainer for your area
  - Yes. CP's can be trainers. Be good at your role and you can be a trainer!
- Suggest ways to be more effective in your area and be innovative!

At the end of your college program, your managers will give you your performance review / evaluation form. This is a form that grades you on your performance during your time as a college program participant. Use this evaluation as motivation to do better and be better. Disney doesn't hold back on these. Even if you think you're a superstar, they're pretty stingy on giving out positive feedback. Many participants receive grades of average and a few marks for above average. But, at Disney, average means you are going above and beyond, so to be above average, you have to REALLY go above and beyond. It may not make sense now, but it will later as you begin to get in your role. Find out what ways you can make yourself stand out at your location and you will be graded positively!

10 MY JOURNEY

I first had aspirations to do the Disney College Program during my junior year in college. My boss at the time had previously worked for Disney and always talked about his adventures. During one afternoon at work, discussing to my peers about internship opportunities, he overheard my conversation and pleaded that I apply for the Disney College Program. I had never heard of it before so I took it upon myself to research the program and discover what it had to offer. I went on to apply that same afternoon, thinking to myself, "why not"?

The next morning, as I woke up for classes, I discovered an email from Disney stating that I needed to complete a web-based interview for my program application. For those who don't know what this is, Disney makes every prospective cast member take this assessment. It's a personality assessment that measures what kind of person you are, how honest you are, and what makes you unique. If Disney thinks the results of your assessment match what they look for in their magical cast members, they will invite you to move on to the next steps of the interview process.

About five days went by and I had honestly forgotten about the application. I was really busy focusing on classes and my part time job at the student center on campus. As I was sitting in class one evening, I got an email from Disney inviting to me to schedule a phone interview for the program. At this point, I began to think it was getting real. Also, it was after this day that the program became all I thought about and it began to take over my thoughts.

I remember a few hours before my phone interview (it was a week later), I was on YouTube looking at previous program participants to seek their suggestions on what to do and what not to do during the phone interview. Some of the biggest things I remembered hearing and doing myself were:

- Smiling when you talk
- Knowing WHY you want to do the program
- Knowing your favorite Disney character(s)
- Knowing and researching what roles you are interested in doing while on the program

As you go through the application process, you will have to select your top choices for which roles you are interested in. Keep these handy, as like I said, you will need these for your discussion during your phone interview.

Again, from earlier in the book, you found out I was in the Fall 2012 Disney College Program and the Spring 2014 Disney College Program. I would like to take the time to go more into detail about my parking program, especially if you happen to get that some role! (You never know)

Fall 2012
Main Entrance Operations (Parking Support)

Being my first program, and my first internship, I was pretty nervous. I had never been to Walt Disney World, so this was all new to me. When I first arrived, the area instantly stole my heart. It was so beautiful, and with the craziness of the drivers, the rush made me feel so alive! I was finally in a big town.

My program started off great (before the work started). My roommate, Manuel, I met online through Facebook. I met him through a friend I met online as well. It's amazing how networking works. Not even knowing who this guy was, I gave him the address to the hotel I was staying at. I figured since he was driving from Dallas, TX to Orlando, FL, he would not only be tired, but hungry as well. I ordered pizza and waited for his arrival.

He finally arrived and it was pretty cool to meet someone who you talked to online. Luckily, we had a lot in common and pretty much spent the first night talking about our lives and what we liked and didn't liked. But, that would be short lived as we had to be up early that next morning to get in line for check in.

On this program, it was different than how it is now. The housing was a first come, first serve basis.

People would get in line as early as 3 and 4 in the morning, trying to get that front spot in line. It was crazy, and Disney actually no longer does this. Either way, we decided to get in line at 5 that morning, and we walked straight over from the Holiday Inn. Once the sun had risen, and the line started moving, the memories began to start.

For starters, once we got in to take our pictures for the housing IDs, the housing staff made both of us go into the restroom to shave. Yes, they literally handed both of us a razor and shaving cream because we were not in the Disney look. Our faces had to be free from any and all hair. I remember we walked into the restroom, only to see about 15 other guys shaving. It was quite hilarious how we had forgotten to shave the night before.

The most awesome moment of check-in was the fact that we got lucky with our housing selection. When we were the next in line to get our keys, we asked for a 1 bedroom apartment in Chatham Square. Not only was a 1 bedroom RARE (it's the most requested), but Chatham was a very nice complex. The magic sat in and the guy told us that there was one left in Chatham and it was ours! We were so excited, plus many of our friends we had met previously through Facebook were staying there as well.

So, enough about all that. Let me talk about my apartment in Chatham Square. I was in 14205. It was a very nice apartment. The only thing I didn't really care for was we had green carpet. Supposedly, we were like the only ones who had green carpet, but it wasn't a big deal. The marble counter tops were beautiful and the fact that the cups and dishes came furnished was very helpful. The noise was always very limited, if none at all. I never had any issues with loud people and the people all around us were very friendly. The bus stop for Chatham was nice because it was actually sheltered for when we had crazy rainstorms.

As far as my experience in my role, it was very rocky in the beginning. Arriving in early September, I was battling the very hot Florida weather. My first few days of working out in the parking lot was intense. Not only was it 103 degrees during my first week, but I also got severely sunburnt on my face and broke out with blisters. How embarrassing. The training was cool, though. (No pun intended… or was it?)

Working for Parking Support was a very different role, that even today, many people get discouraged when they find out that's what they're going to be doing on their program. Well, from experience, I'm here to tell you that it actually isn't that bad. You have to first give it a chance. It's all about your mindset and your attitude. If you walk in with negativity, you will get negative results. If you go in thinking positive, you will get positive results. It's just that simple.

The parking trams were my favorite part of the role. You either got to drive the trams to pick up guests from the parking lot, or you got to talk through the microphone on the back. The scary part during training about the talking part was having to memorize what to say. Disney is obviously all about safety, so you had to ensure you were communicating the right things at all times.

Working out in the parking lot was my least favorite part of the role, but it got better as time went on. See, during the college program, you get scheduled to work a lot of evening/night shifts. More of the senior cast members work during the day. For this reason, I got to work with my fellow CP's (College Program Participants) during my shift. The more I began to feel comfortable with them, the more fun work became. That's why during the book, I stressed the importance of befriending everyone you can and making the most of your relationships with people at work. It is super, duper important.

Halfway through my program, our group in the parking role became very close and we made Sunday nights our social night. House of Blues, as mentioned earlier, turned into an awesome dub-step music rave on Sunday nights, and because it was SIN (Service Industry Night) Disney cast members got in for free! Many of us from work would go together, drink (if you were old enough obviously) and party the night away. Some of the best memories from my program were the nights spent at House of Blues and finding a way to get back home in the morning (joking, but it was fun).

Being away for Thanksgiving was very weird for me. I had never missed holidays before doing the program. Disney made that better for all of us. For Thanksgiving, my area gave us a free Thanksgiving dinner. We were all put into a big SUV, and driven to a cafeteria to dig in! We literally ate Thanksgiving dinner with our managers and that was also a memory I will never forget!

The busiest time of the year was the week of Christmas and the New Year's Holiday. Many of us were scheduled to work doubles on Christmas Eve and Christmas Day, and working 65 hour weeks. Sure, the paycheck was nice, but man were we tired. But, by the time we were working over 40 hours, we were just so thrilled to be working with one another that no one really cared. The job was actually fun and we were working beside our best friends.

The hardest part of the program was the end. Anyone who has completed a college program will tell you tears fall on the last day. That time when everyone has to say their goodbyes, and shake hands for the last time… Those last hugs you will be able to give your friends that worked alongside you for months through the good and bad times... It really is depressing, and many people go back to their hometowns feeling the lingering effects of it. I know I did. It took me a few months to snap out of it when I came home.

That was 2012. It's now 2015 and I still am very in touch with all my fellow parking cast members. It's not a joke when I say you will make lifelong friendships. I look forward to the day that we're all able to have a reunion and go back and discover the memories that we created from our program. It truly was an amazing experience and I'm thankful to have given it a chance. For those looking into doing the program, I challenge you to challenge yourself. Step outside of your comfort zone, and let the world show you how wonderful it can be.

ABOUT THE AUTHOR

Christian Lawrence graduated from the University of
North Carolina at Charlotte with a Bachelor's of Science
in Business Administration. During his studies,
Christian held two internships, with one being at the
world famous Walt Disney World in Orlando, Florida.
Christian was also employed at UNC Charlotte's
Student Union, where he served as a Building Manager
during college. His old boss, Zach, who worked for
Disney, encouraged Christian to do the program to gain
the Disney experience.

Christian was born in Charlotte, North Carolina and is a
huge Carolina Panthers fan. He enjoys learning new
things and meeting new people, and spoiling his cat,
Layna.

Made in the USA
Las Vegas, NV
13 August 2024

93781382R00025